# Beluga Whales

## Animals of the Snow and Ice

Elaine Landau

# Contents

Words to Know ................................. 3

An Animal of the Icy Sea ................. 4

What a Whale! ................................ 6

More About Belugas ....................... 8

Home Sweet Home ...................... 12

Suited for the Sea, Snow, and Ice ...... 14

Time to Dine ................................ 16

Mating Season .............................. 18

Baby Belugas ................................ 20

Hard Times .................................. 24

Save That Whale! .......................... 27

Fun Facts About Belugas ................. 28

Learn More: Books and Web Sites ...... 30

Index ......................................... 31

# Words to Know

**blubber**—The layer of fat under the skin of an animal.

**global warming**—A rise in Earth's temperature. This warming causes climate change.

**mammal**—An animal with a backbone that is warm-blooded and breathes air. Baby mammals are born alive; they do not hatch. Mammals make milk to feed their young.

**melon**—The large bulging forehead of the beluga whale.

**pod**—A group of whales that live and travel together.

**prey**—An animal that is hunted by another animal for food.

# An Animal of the Icy Sea

Picture a huge ice-covered sea near the North Pole. It is always cold there, even in the summer. You are nowhere near home now. You are at the Arctic Ocean.

In the winter, the Arctic Ocean ice is thick and hard. A ship cannot sail on the water. Only submarines can pass beneath the ice.

In the summer, there are still places covered with sea ice. You think that nothing could live here. It is just too cold. Yet some animals are at home in these waters. One of these is the beluga whale. It is an animal of the icy sea.

Beluga whales live in the freezing
Arctic waters.

# What a Whale!

Belugas spend their lives in the water. Yet they are mammals—not fish! That means that they breathe air. They make milk to feed their babies. Baby mammals are born alive. They do not hatch from eggs.

Adult beluga males can grow as long as sixteen feet. That is a little longer than three bathtubs. They can weigh as much as 3,300 pounds. That is more than the average car. Female belugas are big, too. But they are still a little smaller than the males.

All belugas have plump, solidly built bodies. Their heads are small and rounded. These whales have large bulging foreheads called melons. Their melons move and change shape when they make sounds.

Unlike most whales, belugas have neck bones that are not grown together. This allows them to nod and turn their heads. Belugas nod to one another in the water.

Both male and female belugas are big, but the males are slightly bigger.

# More About Belugas

Adult belugas are white. They are not born that way though. They are dark gray at birth. They turn lighter gray as they grow older. Once they are more than six years old, they are all white.

Beluga whales do not live alone. They stay in groups called pods. There can be from two whales to hundreds of whales in a pod.

Baby belugas are dark gray.
Adults are white.

Belugas are very playful and like to chase each other. They will also rub up against one another. These whales can be quite noisy too. Belugas are sometimes called "sea canaries" because they are always making noises. They make lots of different sounds, singing their special songs. Some sounds are like clicks and whistles. Others sound more like a foghorn, or even like birds. The whales use these sounds to communicate and to find food.

Whales live in groups called pods.

# Home Sweet Home

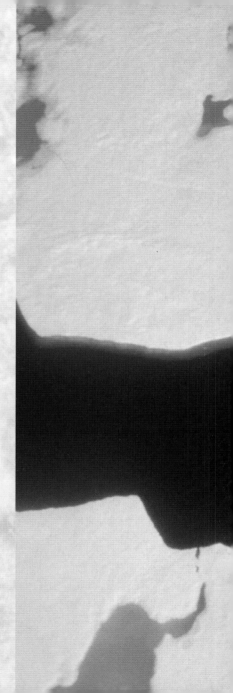

Beluga whales live in the Arctic Ocean and nearby waters. Among these are the Bering Sea, the Gulf of Alaska, the Hudson Bay, and the Gulf of Saint Lawrence. The whales swim among the ice floes. Ice floes are large, floating pieces of ice in the sea.

Some belugas stay in one area all year. Others travel at different times of the year. Thousands of belugas have been seen together on the move.

In the summer, many of the whales swim to shallow bays and mouths of rivers. The warmer river mouths are where they feed and have their babies. Sometimes, they travel up rivers to look for food. Belugas have been seen more than 600 miles up the Yukon River in Alaska.

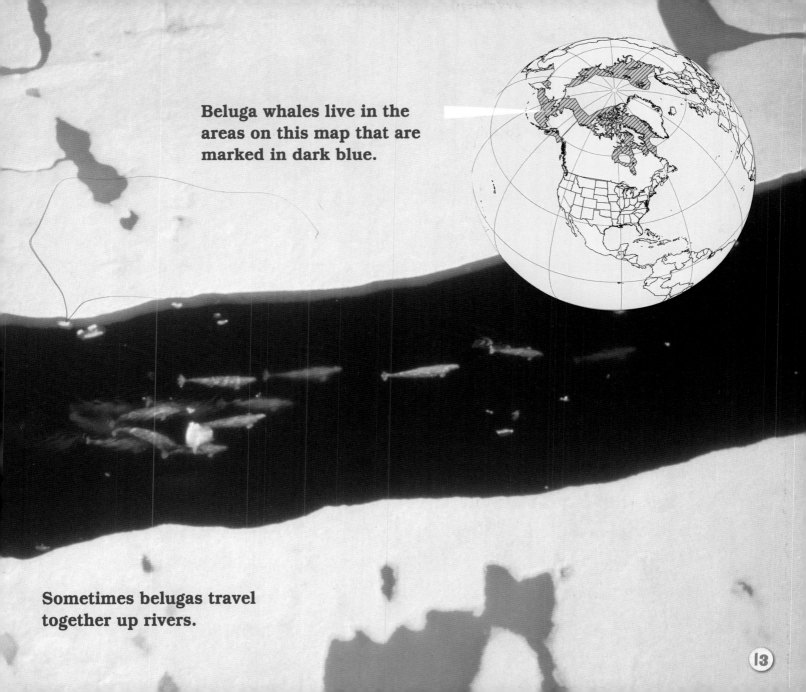

Beluga whales live in the areas on this map that are marked in dark blue.

Sometimes belugas travel together up rivers.

# Suited for the Sea, Snow, and Ice

Belugas are built for icy waters. Unlike many whales, they do not have fins on their backs. They have a dorsal ridge along their backs instead. This stiff ridge helps belugas break through the ice and swim more freely.

Belugas can stay warm in the cold water. They have a thick layer of fat under their skin called blubber. In fact, about half of their body weight is blubber. The blubber keeps out the cold. It also helps keep their body heat in.

Adult belugas are the perfect color for the Arctic as well. Being white lets them blend in with the ice and snow. This makes it harder for their enemies, such as polar bears and killer whales, to find them.

The dorsal ridge on a beluga's back helps it break through ice.

# Time to Dine

Belugas eat more than 100 different kinds of fish and sea animals. Among their favorite foods are salmon, herring, and cod. These fish are rich in fat. Belugas also eat shrimp, snails, clams, and crabs. Belugas eat a lot of squid too. They are sometimes called squid hounds!

Beluga whales often hunt in groups. They use clicking sounds when hunting. The sounds bounce off objects in the water and come back as echoes. This tells the whales where their prey is.

Belugas have 32 peg-shaped teeth to catch and hold their prey. They do not chew their food. They use their mouths and lips to suck in their food.

Belugas have peg-shaped teeth that they use for catching their food—but they don't chew it, they swallow it whole!

# Mating Season

When beluga whales are five to eight years old, they can begin to mate. Mating takes place from late February to early April. Not a lot is known about this behavior in these whales. We do know that the male and female swim together. They let their bodies touch. Then the female swims under the male's belly and the pair mate.

Females give birth the following year from May to July. By then the mothers have carried their babies for fourteen months. The female beluga gives birth to one baby, called a calf. The calf may be born head first or tail first. Adult females have babies every two or three years. When belugas are more than twenty years old, they no longer have babies.

This beluga is giving birth.
Baby belugas can be born
headfirst or tailfirst.

# Baby Belugas

Beluga whales are generally born in the shallow waters of bays and rivers. The shallow waters are warmer than the deep sea. Warm water is important for these young whales. At birth, a calf does not have much blubber. Baby belugas need to feed and grow. When the blubber layer grows thick, it will keep the beluga warm in cold water.

Beluga babies are not too small. At birth, they are five feet long and can weigh nearly 175 pounds. That is about the weight of an adult human male.

Beluga calves usually stay with their mothers for about two years.

21

Belugas can swim at birth. But they still need their mothers. A calf usually stays with its mother and drinks its mother's milk for two years. After one year, the calf's teeth come in. Then it can eat some solid foods as well as drink milk.

Beluga mothers protect their young. The babies swim next to or above their mothers. Often the mothers and their calves form their own pods.

# Hard Times

Belugas face many dangers. Polar bears and killer whales hunt them. Yet today most risks come from humans.

People eat these whales. They hunt belugas for their meat and blubber. Global warming is another danger caused by humans. The Arctic ice is melting more each summer. This could affect water temperature, sea level, and the beluga's prey.

Industry has also hurt the beluga's home. There have been oil spills. Toxic waste has been dumped into the rivers and oceans. Ships can run into these whales and kill them. Noise from the ships can confuse belugas when they are feeding and traveling.

It is getting harder for belugas to live in their waters. One group of belugas lives on the Saint Lawrence River in Quebec, Canada. They have the highest cancer rate from pollution ever seen in an animal in the wild.

Many risks to beluga whales come from humans. This sign, posted by a government office, offers a reward to people who report those who try to harm these whales.

# Help Protect Beluga Whales

## It is illegal to hunt or harass Cook Inlet beluga whales

Help us prevent unlawful harassment, chasing, hunting, or killing of these whales to aid recovery of this depleted population. This will ensure their presence in Cook Inlet for future generations.

REWARD up to $2500

*For information leading to the conviction of person(s) who violate the Marine Mammal Protection Act*

## PLEASE REPORT ANY SUSPICIOUS ACTIVITIES BY CALLING:

NOAA Office for Law Enforcement at (907) 271-3021

NOAA Fisheries HOTLINE at 1-800-853-1964

*All callers can remain anonymous*

NOAA Office for
Law Enforcement

25

# Save That Whale!

People are working to save the beluga. They work with businesses and governments. They find ways to limit the effect people have on the health of these whales.

Laws have been passed to help belugas. Belugas are no longer hunted as much as they once were.

Belugas need clean waters to live in. Steps have been taken to make their waters cleaner. People who pollute rivers and oceans are now punished.

Yet the beluga is still not completely safe. Some beluga populations are decreasing. Belugas are beautiful and wonderful animals. We do not want the world to lose belugas and their special songs.

his beluga whale is being tagged with a transmitter.
cientists will be able to track its location. This will
elp them study the whale.

# Fun Facts About Belugas

* Belugas are slow swimmers. They only swim about two miles an hour. Yet they can still travel thousands of miles.

* An adult male beluga can eat more than sixty pounds of food in one day.

* Belugas can live thirty-five years or more.

* Belugas can swim backward, unlike most whales. This helps them get around ice floes.

* These whales can see and hear well. Scientists think they may not have any sense of smell.

* These whales are sometimes called white whales. The name "beluga" comes from a Russian word for white whale.

* Belugas can hold their breath for twenty minutes at a time. They generally dive three to five minutes for feeding.

* These whales, especially the younger ones, are curious about humans. At times they will swim up to boats.

# Learn More

**Books**

Edina, Julie Murray. *Beluga Whales*. Minneapolis, Minn.: Abdo Publishing Co., 2002.

Rao, Lisa. *Whales*. New York: Bearport Publishing Co., 2008.

Squire, Ann O. *Beluga Whales*. Brookfield, Conn.: Children's Press, 2007.

**Web Sites**

*Cold Water Quest: Beluga Whales*
   http://www.georgiaaquarium.org/animalguide/
   coldwaterquest/belugawhale.aspx

*Whale Times Kid's Page*
   http://www.whaletimes.org/
   whakids.htm

# Index

**A**

Arctic Ocean, 4, 12

**B**

baby belugas, 6, 9, 18, 20, 23
blubber, 14, 20, 24

**C**

calves, 18, 20, 23
color, 8, 14
communication, 10

**D**

dangers, 24
dorsal ridge, 14

**E**

enemies, 14

**F**

female, 6, 18, 23
food, 10, 12, 16, 23

**G**

giving birth, 18
global warming, 24

**H**

helping belugas, 27
human impact, 24, 27
hunting, 16

**I**

ice floes, 12

**M**

male, 6, 18
mammals, 6

mating, 18
melons, 6
milk, 4, 23

**P**

play, 10
pods, 8, 23
prey, 16, 24

**R**

rivers, 12, 20, 24, 27

**S**

sea ice, 4, 24
size, 6
sounds, 6, 10, 16
staying warm, 14, 20

**T**

teeth, 16, 23
traveling, 12, 24

Enslow Elementary, an imprint of Enslow Publishers, Inc.
Enslow Elementary® is a registered trademark of Enslow Publishers, Inc.

**Library of Congress Cataloging-in-Publication Data**

Landau, Elaine.
 Beluga whales : animals of the snow and ice / by Elaine Landau.
   p. cm. — (Animals of the snow and ice)
 Includes bibliographical references and index.
 Summary: "Provides information for young readers about beluga whales, including habitat, eating habits, matin
babies, and conservation"—Provided by publisher.
 ISBN 978-0-7660-3459-4
 1.  White whale—Juvenile literature.  I. Title.
 QL737.C433L36 2011
 599.5'42—dc22

                                2009006478


Printed in the United States of America

082010 Lake Book Manufacturing, Inc., Melrose Park, IL

10 9 8 7 6 5 4 3 2

**To Our Readers:** We have done our best to make sure all Internet Addresses in this book were active and appropriate when we went to press. However, the author and the publisher have no control over and assume no liability for the material available on those Internet sites or on other Web sites they may link to. Any comments suggestions can be sent by e-mail to comments@enslow.com or to the address on the back cover.

**Photo Credits:** © Arthur Gebuys – temp/Alamy, p. 25; Associated Press, p. 19; © Brenna/Shedd Aqua/SeaPics.com, pp. 1, 9; © Flip Nicklin/Minden Pictures, p. 26; Gerald & Buff Corsi/Visuals Unlimited, Inc., p. 32; © Glen Williams/Ursus/SeaPics.com, p. 22; © Hiroya Minakuchi/Minden Pictures, p. 30; © Hiroya Minakuchi/SeaPics.com, p. 11; © John K. B. Ford/Ursus/SeaPics.com, pp. 5, 12–13; National Geographic/Getty Images, p. 3; Shutterstock, p. 17; © Sue Flood/naturepl.com, pp. 15, 21; © Tom & Pat Leeson/ardea.com,  p. 29; © Zigmund Leszczynski/Animals Animals, p. 7.

**Cover Photo:** © Brenna/Shedd Aqua/SeaPics.com

**Enslow Elementary**
an imprint of

 **Enslow Publishers, Inc.**
40 Industrial Road
Box 398
Berkeley Heights, NJ  07922
USA
http://www.enslow.com